CRACKING THE RELATIONSHIP CODE

The Key to Happy Relationships at Home and Work

MERLE M SINGER

AUTHOR
Merle M Singer, merle@relationshipmiracleworker.com

PUBLISHER
eFluential Publishing, info@efluentialpublishing.com

Quantity discounts are available.
To purchase, please contact the author.

Coaching

"Authentic, personable, passionate, confident, and humorous are words that come to mind when I think of Merle Minkoff-Singer. She's developed the perfect formula when relating to people—a no-nonsense approach with a dash of humor and self-reflection thrown in for good measure. She gives it to you straight—and that's why you respect her."

Hellena Jones Elbling, CPCC
Owner/Coach/Change Agent
Core Illuminations

Workshop

"I'm excited to try the various 'exercises' in my work place and feel that they will be beneficial. They will work every day in work and at home. Thank you."

Cynthia Martinez
Greens Coordinator
ABC's *Revenge*

Workshop

"A simple, easy process for creating greater happiness and communication."

Peter Bedard, MA, C.H.T
Convergence Healing

Workshop

"Merle is insightful, informed, and enthusiastic. Her 'take' on relationships is fresh and very effective."

Patti Negri
Owner/Producer
Brain Brew Entertainment

Coaching

"Yes, called you this evening and left a message. Wanted to thank you as my mentor. I remember our last conversation on going forward. I really feel a great sense of accomplishment. Would be great to see you."

EM Vargo

Coaching and Workshop

"Merle Singer's expertise is drawn from her experience with how she navigated through the ups and downs of her own personal and work relationships. This gives her the insight to guide others on how to successfully navigate through their own situations."

EB

Coaching

"Merle Singer has been my mentor for many a year. But for her guidance and encouragement, I would not have been as successful as I have been. She knew exactly how to get me moving."

Ann Hastings
Past International Director
Toastmasters International

Dedication

The person that I dedicate this book to is my husband, Nathan Singer.

First, he brought with him two wonderful children, Ruth and Joseph, now fully grown with partners and children of their own, fully grown. Ruthie can thank Wayne for two wonderful children, George and Amanda and Doris, her partner, for ongoing emotional support. Joseph is grateful to Nancy for their enduring love and their remarkable son, Jacob. In addition, Nathan gave me our wonderful son, Isaac. Thank you, Nathan, for all.

We are celebrating out 50th wedding anniversary this year. Perhaps that makes me a bit more reflective. Nathan taught me that the people who love you the most perfectly are not necessarily the most perfect people. So maybe perfection is not as important as I used to think it was. That's been a hard one for me to swallow. I had even expected myself to be perfect. I still wrestle with that.

I learned that when looking for a spouse, learn to love the one who loves you, rather than teach the one you love to love you. In short, you can't change anyone—except yourself.

In everyday language that means that Nathan has traits in both columns, annoying and endearing. Learning to accept him, not change him, is teaching me to accept me.

The other amazing thing is that what I learned at home holds true in the workplace—different characters, same concepts. And some communication and relationship tricks I learned at work, I learned to use at home. Once you *Crack the Relationship Code*, it works everywhere.

This is what I want to share with you.

Enjoy, learn, share.

Preface

Merle Singer is truly a super woman! I do not say that lightly or often. I am also extraordinarily proud to call her one of my dearest friends in the world. We met over a dozen years ago at a community meeting of some kind in Hollywood. We do also happen to be neighbors and both very civically active. Though I can't remember exactly what the meeting or event was, I do clearly remember my first impression of her. In walks this tiny little spitfire with a shock of purple hair, gorgeously dressed in fabulous oversized artsy jewelry. She walked in and completely commanded the room. Her presence was at least ten times her height. She was awesome. I don't remember what subject she spoke on, but I know she won the crowd over with her clarity, commitment, thoughtful commentary and facts.

Now I am honored to spend five mornings a week with her working out at Lake Hollywood. After our workout, we walk the lake discussing life, humanity, and generally solving all the problems of the world!

As anyone who picks up this book realizes, relationships ARE what makes up and affects everything in the world and in our lives. Humans are relationship people. We need them to survive. But for some reason, they are also one of our most "mysterious" and hard to navigate parts of our lives. This is where Merle is an expert. Besides her education and degrees, the fact that this year she is celebrating her 50th wedding anniversary HAPPILY married to the same man is in itself a testament that she knows what she is talking about.

I have firsthand witnessed her deftly handling a conversation gone awry between lovers, business partners, or friends and neighbors in our workout class. Her techniques and philosophy are simple and proven and anyone can do them to get great results.

I too work with people and relationship coaching, but in a different setting. I am an internationally awarded psychic medium. Yes, I see your jaws dropping. How can some "woo woo" person give credence to anything? Well, I too have been doing it a long time with amazing results, as I work with celebrities, politicians, and business people around the globe ... and what I see in Merle's style is a mirror image of the truths I know and work with—but in an easy-to-understand and digest way that anyone can follow (and not be embarrassed by going to a soothsayer). Give it a go. I promise, this book really can be the answer that you are looking for.

Quick, simple steps to change and improve your relationships—and without even having to even involve the other person. Merle M Singer really is the Relationship Miracle Worker.

Patti Negri
PattiNegri.com
President, AMCPM

Contents

Introduction

Almost everything that we do involves other people, relationship. Yet usually no one teaches us the little tips, tricks, and techniques that would make our interaction with the people in our lives go so much more smoothly. At work, when we have a project to do, the project takes fifteen minutes, but dealing with computer problems (you're on your own on that one) and people problems take a hour or two each.

We don't have time for a degree in psychology or a couple of years of therapy to solve each and every relationship snag with the guy that sits in the next desk at work. And that person that sleeps next to you at home is the person of your dreams—or at least he was. Is it possible that a simple secret technique or two could put back the technicolor in your relationship? There are a few basic concepts that will make all your relationships go smoothly, both at home and at work. Wouldn't you like to know a trick to figure out in advance if he was the right one to marry BEFORE YOU GET MARRIED? Wouldn't you like to know if you should get divorced post haste or give him another chance BEFORE YOU GET DIVORCED? Wouldn't you like to know how to navigate relationship stress at the workplace BEFORE YOU QUIT YOUR JOB?

I have a bachelor's and a master's degree in education and a doctorate equivalent in real-life relationships. This book is being published in the fiftieth year of my marriage to my husband. And yes, we are still talking to each other. It was touch and go around year twenty, but I'll tell you more about that later. I worked for a sheik expanding his holdings in the United States. I sold life and disability insurance and held a Series 7 license to sell investments in addition to insurance. I owned two pharmacies with my husband with up to twenty employees. I raised my husband's kids as my own since they were nine and fourteen and then added a son I gave birth to. And now there are three grown grandkids. I know about relationship from every direction.

In today's society it seems that people are more likely to toss out rather than fix up. That's okay if it's your toaster or computer. It's not necessarily recommended if it's your boss (when you need the job) or your spouse (when you already have kids). Wouldn't it be easier and cheaper if you could figure out a way to be happy in place?

Getting a new job can take from two months to two years. Getting yourself feeling good being single again (even before you want to look at another man) takes a couple of years with the women I know. But wait, it just takes a couple of tweaks in the way you're used to looking at things. Then you can take action. Make yourself happy. And then decide if you want to get married or get divorced or quit your job according to where you are.

These are the tricks, tips, and techniques that I have taught online, in live workshops, and in personal coaching.

It is such a kick when you do your own personal experiment—trying just one of the techniques in this book—and it works. It shouldn't be surprising, but I'm sure you will be. If it takes some tension away from your work day, you will be able to focus more attention on yourself and life at home. I guarantee you that if you read the entire book, you will find at least one technique that will change how you deal with the people in your life and make your life happier. If you don't, email me and I'll send you a refund.

Read the book now, BEFORE you get married, BEFORE you get divorced, and BEFORE you quit your job. Really, isn't your life and the people in it worth the price of this book? Really?

We all can be so grateful of the advancement of technology where we can wish for a book and within minutes be reading it. And please, send me your thoughts to info@relationshipmiracleworker.com. I want to hear your successes. And buy the physical book to give as gifts.

My Story

Do you believe in miracles? You know, "miracle" is defined (3rd definition in Dictionary.com) as a wonderful or surpassing example of some quality. It gives as an example: *"a miracle of modern acoustics." So you see,* I'm not talking about the heavy duty, walk-on-water kind of miracle. I'm talking about the "I've been married coming on to fifty years" when I'm barely forty-five years old yet miracle.

That's how I came to be THE Relationship Miracle Worker. I help women who blame their own unhappiness on their partner. I help them transform their relationship experience and bring more happiness back into their own lives. Yes, indeed; it is a miracle. It was a miracle to me and it's a miracle to each of my students.

To give you a little of my history, I considered myself a modern woman. I wanted it all, and I wanted it perfectly. I wanted the perfect husband, perfect kids, and the perfect house— and even all that wasn't enough. I also wanted a perfect career for me and a perfect art career for my husband Nathan. Then came the Horrific Chimeric Epiphany. It was such a nightmare and with it came a clarity about my future. It was almost twenty years into our marriage. I woke up in the middle of the night in a cold sweat. My dream had not come to fruition—and probably wasn't going to. My brilliant career was not so brilliant and my husband's art was not famous, and there was no white picket fence. It was like going to sleep in Technicolor and waking up in shades of grey (without all the exciting sex).

Was I sad? Was I disillusioned? Yes, underneath it all. But what showed? Anger. Anger to the nth Power. Oh my, I was disappointed. In fact, that's a gross understatement. And, you know, I was embarrassed. There were all those people that I bragged to about how my life was going to be. Where I was going. And as it turned out, where I was going was *nowhere*. I was angry—very, very, very, very angry.

And who was there to be angry at? Who was there? *He was there.* Let's face it—besides everything else, who left his clothes all over the floor? Who left the dishes all over the kitchen counter? Who squeezed the toothpaste in the middle, and who left the toilet seat up in perennial salute? In my mind, it seemed that this man who I had placed all my hopes on had morphed into "Yucky Man," someone who could do no right. Was it a midlife crisis? Was it a lousy marriage? I didn't know which. I didn't know what to do. I needed a miracle.

But here's the thing about miracles. Miracles cannot be pursued. Miracles come (if they do come) when you are busy doing your best. DO is the operative word. I had to DO something. That is when I made one decision that changed my life. First, I made a decision *not to do* some things. Instead of focusing on my husband with his multitudinous foibles, I decided to take him off the pedestal I'd apparently put him on. Really, he just crashed off that pedestal himself. Instead, I put him on the shelf, so to speak. I would deal with him later. What did that mean? It meant we would stay together, for now. I could always divorce him—later. Right now, I didn't want to expend that much energy on him. Instead, I had other things to DO. I did know one thing; I was tired of being grouchy and unhappy and angry all the time.

In my quest for my own happiness, I started focusing on the only person who I had influence over, the only person who always listened to me. ME. Actually, that caused me a bit of a conundrum. At first, I felt guilty and selfish—do you know what I mean? It can be paralyzing. Women are trained as caretakers, at least they were when I was starting out. We women were taught to take care of our husbands, our children, our parents, our community—in fact, everyone EXCEPT ourselves. We are caretakers to the world, but not to ourselves.

A funny thing happened. I had been travelling by plane, I don't even remember where, and the flight attendant's speech stuck out in my mind. It was every flight attendant's speech. "In an emergency, put the oxygen mask on yourself first." And what she didn't add, but could have added, was, "You're no good to anyone if you're dead." Duh, of course it's true. It's not about being selfish; it's about breathing. If you really care about your loved ones, you need to be alive, conscious, able, and functioning. So for sure, you need to take care of yourself first. Another image that may make it clearer for you: "You can't draw water from an empty well." Empty well, empty person. Think about it; it's true. You can't get water from an empty well.

So I started filling myself up. I started making choices that would bring more happiness into my life more of the time. Now I would tell you to make a list of things that you want to do, but at that time I wasn't that conscious. I simply started doing things that occurred to me to do. I joined Toastmasters. I got active in my temple. I became active in the community. I won awards of recognition. These things made me happy. I started to realize that they made me happy, and I focused on consciously achieving happiness—doing more things to purposely make myself happy.

By putting my oxygen mask on first—by focusing on things that would make me happy—I was starting to fill up again. Happiness doesn't just happen; it is achieved. You have to work for it. You have to do something. You can't just stand in the middle of the street with your arms outstretched shouting at the heavens, "Make me happy!" Well, you can do that, but you may just get arrested. What I did, was I did things. Everything I did didn't have to make me happy, just a lot of them. And they did end up producing the exact results I had hoped for. I was happier, more of the time. Yea! I had hoped for it but didn't really believe it could happen. I went from angry to happy. How many can say that? I learned to control my anger. It was a mini miracle. It dawned on me that my anger wasn't the king of me. My anger didn't have to control me—unless I abdicated my control. No more! I was taking charge of my own emotions. Besides, I like me better happy and good natured than grouchy and angry.

At the same time, I noticed other miracles happening. There were unintended consequences—good ones. It was a miracle cluster of *unexpected rewards*. Let me explain. There were four Mini Miracles:

1. I transformed my Relationship Experience with myself; I became happier more of the time.
2. I transformed my Relationship Experience with my husband. He was so grateful for my happy demeanor. I hadn't realized how affected he was by my grouchy mood.
3. It only took one person: me. Nathan wasn't working on himself. He didn't participate. He didn't even realize what was going on, but he was benefitting from my personal efforts at the same time I was benefitting.

4. It is based on universal truths that can work for anyone. For instance, "What you focus on expands." It took me a while to put all that together to create a curriculum for a teleseminar that is being worked into an on-line course.

Miracle #2

The next miracle came with the realization that I changed my relationship experience all by myself; Nathan didn't know, didn't help, didn't agree, and most importantly, didn't care. He just got the benefit and reflected it back to me. Imagine, fixing your Relationship Experience without your partner even knowing. IT ONLY TAKES ONE. Everyone says it takes two to improve a relationship. I've been to couple's therapy. I've been to family therapy. I've been to individual therapy. I've tried to push husband into his own therapy. Everything works; everything has its place.

What works when IT ONLY TAKES ONE is the relief of his non-involvement. You don't have to worry if he will participate. You don't have to worry if he will approve. You don't have to worry if he will improve. You don't have to worry if he will learn. He doesn't even know that anything is going on. And it's all based on *universal truths*. I came to that realization when I did a backward study of my success. I replayed in my head what specific actions I took and what were the specific results. My success wasn't random, but was based on sound universal truths that would work for anyone.

Because my personal success was based on universal truths, I was able to build a course that would repeat my results for anyone who went through the three steps. The course is called "Three Step to Transform your Relationship Experience." I created a curriculum with the help of Jay Aaron, a now-deceased business partner who graduated from the University of Santa Monica with an MA in Spiritual Psychology. I told him what I instinctively did, and he broke it down into more academic language. My years of anger, confusion, experimentation, and success got boiled down into three steps. Simple, fast, easy—this would work for anyone willing to do the steps.

It works in the same way that driving a car is based on simple physical principles that will work for anyone who will turn on the ignition, etc. You don't have to believe that the ignition will start the car for it to start the car.

Here is the 3-Step Curriculum:

- Step One: Your "What Is"
- Step Two: Your "What Could Be"
- Step Three: The Tools for Transformation

Step one is your "what is." In this step, you examine your current interior life. How are you being/feeing on a pretty regular basis? What influences that state of being? What brings you joy and what annoys you—and what does it mean to you? There are worksheets to help you figure it all out.

Step two is your "what could be." This is where you create a simple, powerful vision of what state of being you wish for yourself that's both desirable and believable to you, so that you can wrap your mind and heart around it. You create a unique vision statement. What's unique about this vision is it's about your state of being, not about acquiring specific physical goals. Therefore, you can begin your success instantly. The moment you think a positive thought that makes you happier or calmer or more secure or more confident, you are incrementally more happy, calm, secure, and confident. That's instant success. Your happiness and success is a series of tiny steps that bring you closer and closer to your sense of well-being more of the time. It's all about instant happiness success and the power of tiny steps.

Step three is about the tools for transformation that help you move from your *what is* to your *what could be*. There are seven tools and several worksheets that complete the course.

7 Tools for Transformation

1. Breathe when in stress
2. Take care of yourself FIRST
3. Shift your perspective
4. Appreciating qualities—yours and his

5. Practice not being triggered
6. Take dominion over your anger
7. Experience and express gratitude to self and all 3 Bonus Tools

There are three additional sessions:

1. Worthiness (enhance your own sense of self-worthiness)
2. Accentuate the positive: eliminate the negative
3. Anger: yours and his

There's also a free guided imagery that will give you a sense of how your relationship experience and your happiness could be. Don't undervalue yourself. If there is one error that I see most of us make on a regular basis, it is to undervalue ourselves. We say too often, "Oh, it doesn't matter what I do, if I do, when I do," as if we were not important. We are important. What we do is important. What we learn and share is important.

You can download the free guided imagery at my website when you sign up:

www.relationshipmiracleworker.com/guided-imagery.

What's interesting about the guided imagery is that it gives a reporter's (an outsider) view of a marriage where the partners aren't perfect, but it's not irritating to the wife.

When you see your situation through other eyes, it reminds you of the ½ full part of your relationship. It will give you the oxygen you need to make the changes you need to yourself and your perception to create joy in your life and your partnership. You are worth the effort and maybe your relationship is too.

www.relationshipmiracleworker.com./guided-imagery.

Yea!

Testimonials:

"Even though I've always known if it's to be it's up to me, I find that the exercises and tools you've provided have helped it be for me in a happier and more satisfying way."

"I have very few feeling angry or neglected triggers with my hubby anymore and quite a few feeling appreciated & loved tick marks. In either case, the breathing tool and reminding myself that I deserve to be happy and have the power to choose how I want to feel allows me to let go of the negative and/or embrace the positive."

"I'm getting better at letting negative people and thoughts out of my space and choosing what feels good instead."

"Your advice to look inward and make yourself happy has been driving my actions for well over a month now. I am framing out a new business and no longer looking to him to fill my void; rather, I'm holding him in maintenance mode while I tend to myself for a while. He'll be there when I'm back."

"You've got the knack of teaching through telling stories and showing by example how much your life with Nathan, and his with you, has improved and is getting better the longer you are together."

Before I give specific tips, tricks, and techniques that work in the different situations of "before you marry," "before you get divorced," and "before you quit your job," I would like to tell you a story that will help you in every situation of your life. Every Sunday morning, Nathan and I go to the Hollywood Farmers Market. I get flowers and fruit; Nathan gets vegetable and juice oranges. We live in sunny California, so it's sunny out most days. It's appropriate to wear sunglasses. I wear sunglasses walking past all the stalls. When I come across some peaches that I might like, I look with my sunglasses on, and all the peaches look alike and kind of past ripe. I can't choose a good peach. Then it dawns on me to take off my sunglasses and check out the fruit. Wow, what a difference. I'm able to make a good decision. I tried those orangey lenses. They made everything look too good. In either case, I needed to have clear or no glasses to make a good decision.

What's the point of this story? If you were here, I'd wait for you to answer. But in the book, I'll repeat to you what I'm sure you said. When it comes to relationships, it very important to be aware of what glasses we are wearing. Are we wearing orangey glasses where everything this new man in our life does is perfect? Are we wearing dark glasses where everything our partner does is annoying or evil? Or at work is every thought you have a complaint about something or everything at work? Check your glasses, ladies and gentlemen. Maybe it's not what you see; it's *how* you see.

Section 1

Before you get married

3 Success Secrets to Consider Before You Marry/Connect.

There are 3 important secrets to a happy marriage.
1. Be happy before you even meet him. It requires intention and effort.
2. Who's lucky? You both are.
3. Does he treat you special? Why? How do you treat him?

1. First Things First—Get Happy.

Have you caught yourself in the middle of a thought? What were you thinking? I remember being single, driving home from teaching school, radio on some pop radio program, and thinking, *When I get married I'll really be happy.* Maybe for you that voice in your head said, "When I make my first million I'll really be happy." For me, every wish statement started with "When I get married..." No one told me that it made no sense. No one told me that being happy is an inside job, that no other person can make you happy. So I went about my business and I did get married. I was happy. And one day when we were newly married, and I was driving home from teaching school, radio on some pop radio program, and subconsciously thinking, *When I get married, I'll really be happy*. When I heard myself, it jolted me. I *was* married, and I *was* happy. I just didn't have everything on my list yet. That's when I realized that "when I get married I'll really be happy" had a slightly different meaning for me than the words would convey. To me, it meant I had more things I wanted out of my life. It wasn't that I was not happy; it was that I had more that I wanted to accomplish. Funny how it got expressed in my mind. Have you had the same experience? What is your automatic wish sentence? And what does it really mean to you?

So when you're taking your own Happy Temperature, be aware of your automatic thinking and what it means to you. Then readjust your thinking to be on point. First and foremost, I want to be happy. Only I can make me happy.

Before You Are in Relationship Happy Quiz:

What do I do to make myself happy when I'm sad?

What do you do to make yourself happy when you're sad? Are there things you do when you're blue? Singing, dancing in the kitchen, reading a book, going for a walk. Do you have something? If not, create something that works in your life, and label it Happy Times; then use it every time you feel a bit down. If it doesn't lift your spirits, find another activity and keep trying till you find your Happy Times.

If you can hone this skill so that you maintain a happy frame of mind most of the time, then you can feel assured that you will make and find a good partner. And you'll have the confidence to win and keep him. Trust me, to keep a man, you need to be happy. Women worry about being sexy enough, smart enough, pretty enough, but I haven't ever heard a woman worrying about being happy enough to make a man happy. Most men, most healthy men, do not like perpetually unhappy women or partners. Many men who cheat on their wives are looking for a woman who is happy or who they can make happy. Well, we'll get more into that later.

If you are married, ask yourself, "What do I expect my partner to do when I'm unhappy?"

What do you expect your partner to do when you're unhappy? He doesn't have to do anything. It's not his job to make you happy. But if flowers would make you happy, ask him to bring home flowers, and like whatever kind he brings. Please don't tell me that he's supposed to know to bring you flowers. No he isn't. Other people can't read your mind—at least not on a regular basis. There is nothing wrong with reminding him when it's your birthday or when you just would like a box of candy. He will love that you gave him the tip. Of course, that depends on how you asked him. It's not always what you say, it's often how you say it. Partners want to make you happy even if it's not their job. When they try, be appreciative even if it isn't quite what you would have bought.

Have you ever felt in kind of a funk and asked yourself why you felt like that? Is your personal life bad? Is your job bad? Has your car broke down? Don't be surprised if you answer yourself "no" each time. Sometimes we simply have a funky mood habit. We don't really have a bona fide reason to be down. It's just become a habit.

This is your opportunity to practice intentional thinking instead of subconscious, default thinking. Practicing this is like spiritual exercise. The more intentionally happy you are and the more appreciative for it you are, the more prepared you are for a happy marriage and partnership. Most people have it backward. So often they jump into a relationship to make themselves happy instead of making themselves happy so they are prepared to create a happy relationship. And remember, part of being happy is being grateful—

> So often they jump into a relationship to make themselves happy instead of making themselves happy so they are prepared to create a happy relationship

grateful that you have a partner who even tries to make you happy.

JayJay told me she was very happy. She had a great job. She made good money. She had friends. She didn't have a romantic relationship, but she had a fabulous dog that kept her company and gave her love. She was ready for a romantic relationship, but she worried to me that it was too late; she was almost fifty. It did seem like it might be too late. It was a year or two of being on top of the world, but by herself, when, voilà, Mr. Right appeared. It's just amazing how it happens.

You know, not everyone is cut out for married life. It takes some sacrifice and adds some bonuses. If it's been more than two years since you've declared yourself open to entering a romantic relationship, and no one has appeared to sweep you off your feet, that is a clue for you to do some deeper soul searching. There may be some things deep inside you that you haven't dealt with yet. You have two choices: 1) you can continue as you are, single and satisfied, or 2) you can do some self-exploring questions to unravel the remnants of old hurts or confused thinking. It's like digging for gold—a lot of work and rich rewards.

2. The Lucky One: Which One Is It—Him or You?

Relationship is the only thing we do our entire lives. We

"Think about thinking about what you're thinking about your future relationship."

interact with other people from infancy to death. Yet we give it so little thought. Then all of a sudden when we are contemplating marriage—I mean, even before we have anyone specific picked out—we start thinking about relationships and how they work, what makes a good one and such. How we think about this relationship, even before we are in one, will make a difference with what kind of relationship we gravitate toward. For that reason, "Think about thinking about what you're thinking about your future relationship." Don't take for granted what you are thinking. Be purposeful and aware.

Here's an example. A young woman sees a young man about town and she thinks to herself, *Boy would I be lucky to catch such a great guy, but he wouldn't look at ugly, plain, flat-chested, dumb me.* Even if she does land him, she will never be an equal partner thinking the way she does. And she would be ripe for spousal abuse. What if the young woman sees another young man about town and she thinks to herself, *Now that's a guy I can get because he is so ugly, plain, bony, and dumb.* Even if she does land him, she will never let him be an equal partner to her thinking the way she does. And she would be ripe for abusing her spouse. Let's face it, if it's to be a successful marriage, both partners are lucky. In good partnerships, you will sometimes hear them say to each other, "I am so lucky to have you." They are appreciative and grateful. Are you appreciative for what you have in your life right now? That's the place to start.

3. Who Does He Treat Special?

Let's face it, if it's to be a successful marriage, both partners are lucky.

As a matter of fact, there are many ways we think about things that seem like common sense. And yes, they are common; but no, if you explore a little more deeply, they do not make sense.

Here's an outrageous secret I wrote about in my first book, *The Valentine Relationship Book*, so counterintuitive at first: **Make sure he's NOT just treating *you* special.** That sounds really odd, but hear me out (or 'read' me out).

If you're not married yet, this is a very important tip. And if you are married, it may help you reevaluate your partner. Make sure that he is NOT (I repeat, NOT) "treating you special."

Everybody tells you to make sure he *does* treat you special while you're dating, while he's courting you. That's what my mother said to me. And when I came home and told her that I had found the one I wanted, I remember that conversation to this day. "Does he treat you special," she asked. "No," I answered my mom, "he does NOT treat me special. He treats me great, but he treats everyone great. He's a very nice man." Before my mother, with that quizzical look on her face, could say, "Yes, but..." I continued: "What a mistake that would be to be taken in by some man who treated me like a 'queen.' Men who treat you special are often on a self-serving assignment, a conquest. They have a mission; the mission is to capture your heart and/or your body.

When they capture your heart/body, their mission is fulfilled. They're done. There's no reason to treat you special any more. I'm sure you've heard of so many cases, when confused and unhappy women bemoan the fact that their partner hardly even notices them, let alone treats them special anymore.

I continued, talking to my mom: "I am so reassured that he treats me the way he treats everyone in his life, and he treats everyone with caring and consideration even though it comes out of his gruff, masculine manner." Because he treated me just like he treated everyone else, I felt confident that he would continue treating me well even after the bloom was off the rose—and our life would settle into the eventual predictability that some confuse with monotony.

It was one of the few times that my mother didn't argue back. She listened and showed respect for this new idea. It turns out I was right this one time. It's been fifty years that he's been treating me NOT special. Although, it turns out I have felt pretty special, except for that time around our nineteenth year of marriage when I went through my midlife crisis and was sure that *he* was the cause of my misery. Ah, but that's another story for another time. Check out "My Personal Valentine Story" toward the end of the book for more details.

So pay attention to your man. How does he treat the other people in his life? Would you want to be treated the way he treats his mother, his buddies, his business colleagues, the waitress? And by the way, flirting with the waitress is not the same as being respectful of the waitress. Is he respectful, thoughtful, loving to the important people in his life? That's how he will treat you when you are an important person in his life.

However you want to be treated, make sure he is treating others that way. You see, how he treats you, tells you about HIM. It doesn't tell you about you. It doesn't tell about how wonderful you are; it tells you about him and how wonderful he is. Grab him; he's a keeper.

And just in case he doesn't treat you well, that doesn't mean you are unworthy, because you *are* worthy. I know because you're taking the time and the effort to read this, regardless of how imperfect you are. If he treats you great, it doesn't prove you're great—although you *are* great. All people who read my books are great—and also have a sense of humor.

The 'I Deserve Respect and Love' Test

You know, we women are all too eager to believe that we deserve what we get even if it's bad. I have a test that you can take to see if you do deserve his kindness and consideration. You must remember, that it goes for both partners.

Here's the Test Question: ***How well do you treat the people in your life?*** If you are treating someone, anyone, with little or no respect, it has nothing to do with them even if they are vagrants sleeping on the street; it has to do with you and how you treat the people in your life. And how you treat the people in your life has everything to do with how deserving you think you are and, conversely, how you treat yourself.

You Deserve Respect—So Does He

If you are in a relationship where you feel you are not getting the respect that you hope you deserve (and I tell you that you *do* deserve that respect), I suggest that you pay close attention to how you are treating your partner (and everyone in your life). Make a concerted effort to be respectful, kind, compassionate, and gentle and ***choose not to be angry***. ANGER IS A CHOICE; DON'T CHOOSE IT. Do that for, say, twenty-one days, and see if there are changes in the way your partner behaves with you.

Is It Time to Move On?

If he is still unkind, it's not you. It's not your fault, and it may be a signal to you to move on without him. But speak to someone (not everyone) about it—a clergyperson, a psychologist, psychiatrist, coach, counselor, a wise, uninvolved friend. Find someone in your life to work through this with you. You are strong enough and smart enough to get help, to bring people onto your team to help you work through this.

The short of it is this: If you want to be treated specially, find someone who treats everyone specially. That's your "special" insurance policy.

I want to put an addendum on that story. I was talking with a friend about my "special" theory, and he took umbrage. He looked over at his wife of thirty-five years, and with love in his eyes said, "I still treat her special."

What's interesting to me is that I know this couple for a long time, Bartram and Sallyanne. I talked about my "treat you special" theory. He disagreed with me. He said he always treated his wife special and these thirty-five years later, he still treats her special. Sallyanne is a lovely person who treats her Bartram with love and respect. Bart used to be much grouchier as a younger man. I remember. The change in him was so subtle, and over such a long period of time, that I didn't even think about it until we had this conversation. It seems that his love for his wife mellowed him and expanded his view of people and life. He started out with a clear prejudice against the gay lifestyle, but mellowed to where he lovingly supported his own gay daughter and her partner. His support of his wife has enabled her to do wonderful non-profit work. They are happy. I think in this case, Bart did treat his wife special and learned from her how to treat everyone with more patience and respect. What I see as key to their success is their mutual respect and gratitude for each other and their life together. What's kind of neat to observe from the sidelines is that it brings out the best in each of them and, of course, it enhances the relationships with their children and grandchildren.

So there are three things that you have in your life and in your consciousness when you embark on the quest for a life partner. If you are both happy, it means that you are both independent. You are each living a life that you have created on your own. That brings so much confidence to you that when it comes to the second point, who is lucky, you can easily answer that each of you are lucky. If you are lucky on your own, and you still choose to be together, you will be luckier together and you'll know to be appreciative. Then, when it comes to number three, does he treat you special, the answer will be that he treats everyone with respect and appreciation; then, if he treats you even more special, it will be for good, loving reasons.

There are a few other things that will hold you in good stead that I will mention in the next session, including adding humor and subtracting name calling.

Section 2

Before you get divorced

The Relationship Valentine Book: Three Outrageous Secrets You Simply Must Know.

You can find my book on Amazon
http://tinyurl.com/anrcqzp

Before I get on the topic of No Name Calling, I'd like to make one observation. If you are a name caller, you know it's true. If you are called names, please know that while the names shouted out are meant to hurt, they are not necessarily the true feelings of the shouter. So if he calls you a slut, he doesn't believe that, he just knows it will hurt you. And if you call him a fat slob, it doesn't mean you don't love him as he is, it means you know it will hurt him to call him that. And why do we want to hurt each other? We're angry.

We'll deal with anger later on. Suffice it to say here that letting out your anger doesn't dissipate it; it expands it.

I've talked about your partner treating you special. But first he has to learn and believe that he too is special. And you do too, by the way. I saw a movie a couple of years ago, Birdman. It was truly a graphic, surreal story of a man plagued by his own insecurity.

I've seen surreal paintings (Dalì), but this was the first surreal movie I'd ever seen. (I don't do horror films.) Michael Keaton's character was breaking glasses across the room by simply pointing his finger or flying through the air like the Birdman, the part he played that made him famous.

I don't make it my job to review the movies, but I enjoy using it to talk about relationships. It is my belief that the rock solid foundation of any love relationship is a strong ego. **We have to believe in ourselves or we won't be able to believe anyone could love us. Or else we think that anyone who loves us is inadequate in some way, and so we treat them like doo-doo (the scientific word for poop).**

We all have voices in our heads that chatter at us all our waking hours. It's why we all need sleep—to temporarily escape the voices. Well, then we dream. That's why meditation and yoga-type activities are so important, because they teach us how to control the voices when we are awake.

Michael Keaton's character has one mean, nasty voice in his head. Having to live with that your whole life is like having to be in prison. The saddest thing about this main character is that he has misidentified the voice in his head. He thinks the voice is telling him the truth, but that is so far from the truth that it's the opposite.

How can I explain this? I tell you that the mean voice is a saboteur/betrayer trying to keep you from being your best self, trying to keep you small and unconnected from what makes you special and significant.

Each of the characters had these insecurities, but Michael Keaton's internal conflict was surreal. The surrealism was a theatrical construct, whatever that means, that puffed up the pain of his self-doubt to the huge proportions of the superhero he once played. The battle within him was reality for him.

The main character was so plagued with these negative feelings that he needed all his energy to nurse his own ego and left him precious little time, insight, or inclination to notice or interact or care about anyone else—except on a very limited basis like the music in the background of his soul, or whatever that is.

But what has all this got to do with you? All the arts are a mirror held up for us to look at ourselves. And what do you see? Do you question why anyone would love you? Do you honor that love?

If you are having relationship issues and are confused about how to handle them, you may email me at info@relationshipmiracleworker.com for one free half hour session.

Dr. Phil McGraw says, "I think people in America get divorced too quickly. I think they do it too easily. I think it gets to the point where they say I'm not having fun anymore; I quit."

I happen to agree with Dr. Phil McGraw of the Dr. Phil Show. People aren't willing to put the work into their marriage, but they have no idea how much work it is to be divorced. Life takes work—married or living, together or divorced, straight or gay—it takes work.

Here's an example. Create a Happy Environment. I've told you that I was happy. I'm not a reclusive happy; I'm a social happy with whomever I'm with. And guess who I was with when I got home each day. Of course, it was "Hubby Poo" (the former "Hubby Shmoo"). It's in the eye of the beholder. Nathan hadn't changed. He just looked better in the brighter light of my own happiness. Who got the benefit? Nathan didn't understand what was going on, and he didn't care. He was loving it. I did all the work and everyone around me—AND ME—got the benefit.

> Nathan hadn't changed. He just looked better in the brighter light of my own happiness.

I call that The Happiness Responsibility. I wasn't relying on him for my happiness. It was Compound Happiness. I *learned* that focusing on my own happiness had the *intended* consequence of changing my relationship experience with myself, and the *side benefit/unexpected reward* was that it also transformed my relationship experience with my husband. That made him happy, and so he reflected back his happiness. It's compounding happiness, the ping pong effect. When I was happy, I was nice to Hubby. That made him happy, so he did things to make me happy. It worked; I was happy, and back at him. Ping pong, ping pong, ping pong.

The Tiny Experiment, The Big Effect

It started out as a tiny experiment, and became a grand wonderful experiment that turned our marriage of twenty years—that had become questionable—into fifty years of bliss. Don't get me wrong, bliss includes a few arguments, a few disagreements, a few complaints. My eyes still flash occasionally. We're still ping ponging our way through life together. That was My Very Own Miracle. It was the first relationship miracle that I experienced, my own. IT ONLY TAKES ONE.

> the work that it takes to save your marriage is the work that you will have to do anyway when you are divorced.

What's really interesting is that the work that it takes to save your marriage is the work that you will have to do anyway when you are divorced. You see, the work you have to do is on yourself. It has nothing to do with him or her or anyone else. You (working on yourself) is your first job. Are you mad at me for saying that? Or are you just mad? Make absolutely no important decisions when you are angry. I know you may be saying, "I see clearly for the first time..." (usually followed by something negative). In reality, we do not see clearly when we are angry. We see our world through dark, angry glasses. When you're first in love, you see things through rosy glasses. With a little work on yourself, you'll be able to see things through clear glasses.

So the question is what kind of work do you have to do on yourself to see the world through clear glasses? This is the best kind of work. Your mission, should you choose to accept it (à la Mission Impossible) is to make yourself happy. "Ridiculous," you say. But no, it is not ridiculous and it is not impossible. And if you surrender yourself to the possibilities, it may be lots of fun. Oh, so you want to know why you should even bother? What does it have to do with the creep and how fast I can ditch him? The answer is easy; it's all about the glasses.

When you are angry and wearing dark glasses, everything looks dark. Look, I've already told you, when I go to the farmers market, I take off my sunglasses to look at the peaches and see their true vibrant color. It makes a difference. I can't see the produce clearly enough to make a decision on whether I want to buy a particular apple or tomato until I take off the dark glasses and look at their "real" color. In the same way, being unhappy is perpetually wearing dark glasses.

Now you tell me that as soon as you ditch him, you'll be happy. If your happiness depends on anyone else doing anything, that's not happy. Happy comes from within. Victor Frankl found that out in a Nazi concentration camp, when they stripped him and burned the only copy of his precious manuscript that he had poured in so much of himself to write, and then made him give up his thin marriage ring standing there naked. His refusal to hate them and boil in anger, his *triumph,* was his control of his own feelings. The Nazis could completely control his physical life, but he would not let them control his inner life. My, how strong Victor Frankl was. For me, just writing about it could bring me to anger if I let it. If you are letting someone anger you so much that you are arguing with some faceless author (not really, I'm on the back cover), you are being controlled by another. Someone else can control you physically, but no one can control your emotions without your permission.

What I'm suggesting is to change the order in which most people do things. Usually people get unhappy, blame the relationship, divorce, find they are still unhappy (just no more screaming). That's when they start analyzing the situation and see a bit more clearly how things were. By then it's too late to go back, so they just have to take the lessons they've learned (if they have learned any lessons) to their next relationship. Only the one important lesson they may have never learned is to see, without dark glasses, what's going on and decide if what they really want is divorce.

Maybe the timing is perfect for you reading this book. Maybe you have barely enough patience to try out just one more thing before you divorce. But what should you do? *Let's face it, he's never going to change. What's the point?* The point is that he doesn't have to change, which is a good thing because you are right; he is never going to change. At least you can't make him change. There is one interesting thing, though. The interesting thing is that even if he doesn't change, he will behave differently in a different environment. People act differently in different circumstances. If you make his situation different, he won't change, but he will behave differently. But never mind for now. Right now we are angry at him and could care less about how he feels or acts.

When people are angry, it is either due to sadness, disrespect, or frustration. Take a moment here and write down why you are angry. And by the way, notice if you are even angry at *him*. Maybe you are really angry at the boss or your mother or the kids, or your best friend, or yourself. Maybe it is a mixture. But take the time to figure this out because you will need to deal with it to release your anger. So what I'm saying is that you have to release your anger and bring happiness back into your life before you can make an effective decision about anything.

This can be very easy to release just by realizing the true cause of your anger. Or maybe you are used to being angry and are afraid that you won't have the courage to say all the things that he/she has done to wrong you. I remember saying to myself, "I have to keep this anger till I see him and tell him what he did that was so wrong." Now that may not make sense to me now, but it sure made sense to me then. My anger served me. It was my courage. It was my mouth. It was my moral compass. That's how I saw my parents cope. Listen to me making excuses for myself. I remember feeling insecure and not as strong as my husband, so I used my anger like liquor or drugs to give me strength to argue.

When I got angry enough, I suggested we separate. It was our kids that slowed that down, by asking us to get therapy first. The therapy did make Nathan a bit more sensitive to my needs and more aware of what he could do, but I wasn't any happier.

I had to forge a new path for myself. I had to figure out what would make me happy. I could have done that after I got divorced, but that would have been very disruptive and would have delayed my working on myself. Hey, now there's a thought: are you staying mad at your partner and filling your life with divorce proceedings in order to delay working on yourself? Just remember you can't avoid this cold, hard look at your inner self. You can only delay it. And that delay has a serious, real-life heavy price. You are destroying a marriage or partnership that may not be the true cause of your discontent.

It may be hard for you to see. Because you are looking at him being wimpy or thoughtless or spineless or sloppy or all of those things. How could you ever want to be with him for one more moment? I don't know. Maybe you wouldn't. But maybe you would. You did marry him. You did make a life with him. Maybe he's redeemable.

But frankly it doesn't really matter at this point. You're not even ready to make those decisions. Right now, it's all about your glasses. What do you have to do to ditch the dark glasses? But wait, let me correct one statement that I made. I said, "You can't avoid this cold, hard look at your inner self." That's wrong. Some people do avoid that cold, hard look at themselves. They live the rest of their lives justifying themselves, defending their victim status, very content in their anger and unhappiness. So that is an option for you, too, if you want to choose it for yourself.

I'm counting on you making a better choice. After all, I rate my readers as highly evolved. Life without anger (or minimal anger) is a worthy goal. That creates more room and energy for getting more stuff done. Stuff that makes you feel good about yourself. Maybe you'll write a book, or read another book, or volunteer at a worthy charity---so many opportunities.

I have been married for fifty years. If that doesn't impress you, it impresses me. First of all, how old must I be to be married that long? It's beyond my comprehension. The other amazing part is that although my marriage is lovely and fulfilling and fun now, it wasn't always so. Most marriages, if not all have their ups and downs. If I had been impetuous during a really down time. I'd have been gone. At the behest of our son, we tried therapy. And that really was my great awakening. The awakening came from what worked and what didn't. Maybe it wasn't the marriage that was not working; maybe it was me. That, it turns out, was a brilliant conclusion.

What was wonderful about it, was that it put my life, my happiness, in my own hands. At the time, I decided to allow the marriage to glide along as it was, and to concentrate on my own happiness. I could always get divorced later if I wanted. The problem was that I didn't know what to do to make myself happy. The best I could think of was to do things that I had previously thought about doing, but never got to. I joined Toastmasters to improve my public speaking and build my confidence. I called the rabbi in my synagogue and asked to join a particular committee I had always been interested in. I started a neighborhood watch program near where I lived. All of those things expanded beyond my wildest dreams. In Toastmasters, I accomplished getting Distinguished Toastmaster designation, which is pretty high. At my temple, I ended up becoming president. In my Hollywood neighborhood, I eventually became civilian co-chair of the Hollywood Community Police Advisory Board for several years. I felt good. I was happy. I could see where I was making a contribution. I would come home from work and say "Hi, Honey" with my voice lilting. The first time I did that, Nathan looked at me in disbelief, with a "Who is this woman?" look on his face.

That's when I realized it wasn't him; it was me who had been spreading misery. I had unrealistic, fairytale expectations of marriage, expecting him to meet my needs, when clearly that was my job. I had to stop telling him how to live and what to do and start telling myself how to live and what to do.

> I had to stop telling him how to live and what to do and start telling myself how to live and what to do.

In 1998, I won Distinguished Woman of the Year Award from the Hollywood Chamber of Commerce. I was concentrating on my own contributions to this world.

Armed with a new self-satisfaction, I felt good about myself now. It was interesting how I saw me being angry at my husband for whatever I decided he didn't do. And whatever they tell you about visualizing what you want, remember that's only the beginning. You have to take steps to get your dream. I wanted to see my husband clearly. What was he really like?

Now he looked different. He hadn't changed. I just saw him with compassion instead of anger. Isn't it interesting that I had been angry at him because I wasn't happy? Am I the only one who, if I examined my own thoughts very deeply, expected my husband to live his life in a way that would make me happy?

It sounds ridiculous when I write it out like this, but it's how I really thought. If he had been more focused about selling his artwork. If he had become a famous artist. That would make me happy. But maybe it wouldn't have made me happy; maybe it would have made me feel left behind. So if his being famous couldn't guarantee my happiness, then his not being famous couldn't cause my unhappiness. It wasn't fair for me to ask anyone else to be in charge of my happiness. I really didn't want that. I was just too scared that I couldn't make myself happy. I was afraid I would fail at whatever I tried. It was easier to focus on him and disrespect him for not moving his career to fame and fortune. What was more unforgivable to me was that he simply didn't have the drive to create a career. He was happy loving his family—me, the kids, and the grandkids. That's what was the ultimate annoyance; he was happy with his life. As long as I was reasonably happy and loving to him, and the kids were fine, his life was and is right on course. If that wasn't enough for me, that was on me. I needed to write a book or something, which of course was scarier than being angry at him.

> That's what was the ultimate annoyance; he was happy with his life.

This is a synopsis of my life starting at the twentieth year of our marriage. I could so easily just have made 'the big change,' divorce. As I teetered on the brink, there was one thing that was the tipping point. I could always get a divorce. It wasn't a now-or-never situation. My husband wasn't abusive or violent or threatening. He was more wounded and sad. What I did that was smart was that I wasn't abusive to him either. I might have been snippy, but I was controlled. If I had been nasty, I would have burnt my bridge back to him.

I am a firm believer in keeping all options open until you are firm on the appropriate choice. So that brings up the whole question of how do you make life-changing choices? I have some thoughts about that. If you can't make a decision without muttering curse words under your breath, or out loud, I recommend you delay your decision. If you are absolutely sure that your mood changing won't change your decision, I have a story you may relate to.

I used to smoke. I started when I was 19. My mother smoked. She had a coca cola every morning (no coffee) and a cigarette—mostly Pall Malls. So, of course, as a child, I always thought smoking was cool.

I smoked for 10 years, and my mental picture of people smoking was positive. At 29 and again at 31, I stopped smoking. When I stopped, people that still smoked no longer looked cool to me. My mother smoked till 68 and developed emphysema. It just wasn't cool. And the people I saw smoke seemed low class and uneducated, not quite as clean from all the cigarette stink. All of that took place in my head, and I know I'm not the only one. I changed my perception of smoking 180 degrees. Our mind is powerful. Harness that power for your own benefit. And it will benefit everyone around you.

Trust me, Nathan looked a heck of a lot different to me after I had focused on myself and made myself happy. He hadn't changed; I had. But wait, let me revise that last sentence a bit. He hadn't changed, but how he behaved did change in a way. You see, he was dealing with a different environment—meaning me and how my mood was and, therefore, how I treated him. I was happier. That made him happier. I was nice to him; he went out of his way to do things to please me. I acknowledged and thanked him for his thoughtfulness, and he felt successful and happy. If your life is going to spiral, this is a great way for it to spiral—upward.

There are a couple of things that I concluded about married life that no one ever told me before.

Here's the miraculous conclusion I came to that I had never heard anyone ever say before: IT ONLY TAKES ONE. My husband didn't do a dang thing. He didn't know what to do. I did everything. And pretty much, I did everything for me, to make me happy. And I was ready to check out of the marriage if I thought that it would have made me happier. I just didn't think it would make me happier than I was making myself right here where I was. And look at the aggravation I saved myself: would I lose my step-kids (even grown), how would we divide our assets, what choices would our friends make? Our parents were gone, so that wouldn't be an issue. Divorce is messy. I've watched my friends. When it's the right thing to do, it's the right thing to do. But it turned out it wasn't right for me. I know some of you are saying that I'm lucky that my husband wasn't cheating on me. If he's cheating on you, you have no choice. That's a complicated issue. Men cheat for different reasons. Short of abuse (verbal or physical), I recommend working on yourself where you are. If you divorce him, you will have to work on yourself anyway, so why not start now, right where you are? This way, you can concentrate on what presently makes you happy. And you won't have the added pressure of how you will support yourself, how you will split the kids (and sometimes that's just how it seems). Why not figure those things out before you make a move? If you really focus on doing things for yourself and making yourself happy, you will give yourself the advantage of seeing your hubby and marriage with clear glasses. If you made yourself happy, for sure you would have a happy aura. Happy people are always obvious, and people like to be around happy people. As you 'happify' yourself, you will not only see your husband differently, he will see you differently. The vibe around your relationship will change, including the kids. Even if you still decide to divorce, the process will be calmer and easier on everyone, including the kids.

You may feel guilty focusing so much attention on yourself and your own happiness. How selfish that seems. I felt strange about it at first, but this is what I came to realize. Quite often guilt is not about doing something wrong, but about doing something different. We feel guilty in order to mask the fear of change. It's like doing push-ups. Assuming we are healthy, doing push-ups will expand our health, but it hurts when we start. Then it doesn't hurt until we get to ten, to twenty. We determine how many push-ups we do (unless we're in the Army), and even then we still made the choice. We chose to join the Army.

So be careful when a feeling of guilt stops you from doing something that isn't illegal or very hurtful to someone else. And be careful when you do things for other people so you won't feel guilty. It's taken me a lifetime to learn to say no to food I don't want just so I won't hurt someone's feelings. Taking or not taking that piece of cake is on me. Feeling good or bad about what I do is on me. Feeling hurt that I didn't try the cake is on them. That gremlin of the status quo will resort to any argument to keep us stuck where we are. Better to feel scared than to feel guilty. And fear may be your constant companion. You just will be able to move forward in your life if you put fear at the back of your caravan of emotions. If you must bring fear with you, don't let it lead you. You are your own leader in your life. And remember, scary is just another word for exciting, energized, and forward-moving. If you are still feeling guilty, remember you can't get water from an empty well as we discussed in chapter one.

So what does this all amount to? Most important, *it only takes one* to change a relationship. This is the most important thing I have to say. Even if you are already on your fifth relationship, even if you only take one thing away from this book, remember: *It only takes one to change a relationship.*

I can already hear you explaining that your husband, your partner is worse. *He's incorrigible. He is cheating on me. He is dead sexually.* I can hear you saying how you've done everything and it's done.

Here's my answer to you: "Okay, okay. It's done. So relax. Don't try to change him, awake him, or *anything* him. It's not about him. It's about you. You don't have to leave him—yet. Maybe you will—later."

It may sound bizarre to think that concentrating on yourself and making yourself happy can save your marriage. It's all about going inside instead of outside. Going outside means not changing anything about yourself and going outside to find someone else. That's called cheating. Yes, I know, he may already be cheating. But remember, it's not about him; it's about you. Cheating doesn't solve the problem; it masks it. Even if you have this fabulous relationship with a single man so you don't mess up someone else's relationship. You fall in love with Guy#2. You get married to #2. We won't even get into all the lives you disrupt. You get married. You settle in. Issues arise. With this guy also. The problems are a little different, but there are still problems. Frankly, it all may be worthwhile if it's the right decision. However, even more second marriages end in divorce than first marriages.[1] Statistics show that in the U.S., 50 percent of first marriages, 67 percent of second, and 74 percent of third marriages end in divorce.

Do yourself a favor. Check in with yourself. Having an affair may make you feel like a TV series, but this is your life. In real life, there is fall out from disrupting another family regardless of what he says is going on in his marriage. I know he makes you feel loved and lovable and important. Those are wonderful feelings that everyone should have. HOWEVER, start with yourself. If you want to be loved and lovable, volunteer. If you want to be loved and lovable, love yourself.

Number Three, A successful marriage is not a conflict-free marriage. Everyone has arguments. Everyone's partner is a pain in the neck. In fact, everyone who isn't you is a pain in the neck, and let's face it you're not so sure of you sometimes. Just today, someone was complaining to me about how her husband loads the dishwasher. Hilarious. Why is it so funny? Because my husband already knows not to even try to load the dishwasher. I have willingly stopped complaining about his leaving dishes on the counter, just so I get to load

---

[1] https://www.wevorce.com/blog/why-do-second-marriages-fail/ Jan 9, 2017

the dishwasher myself, the "right" way. I learned that it's better to do some things myself and not complain. Cause let's face it, some things he just can't do right. Ask Nathan; some things I just can't do right. Couples are hilarious. Just listen to them and say nothing. Each couple has their particular way to accommodate each other. But rest assured each partnership has some tension, because we are all imperfect people. Please, don't be looking at other couples and thinking how wonderful they are together. You very well may be right, but that doesn't mean that they don't ever get on each other's nerves every once in a while. Relax, you may have it better than you realize.

I want to tell you the story of Shanna. Shanna was married to a successful doctor. It was her third marriage. She had children from two other marriages. This man embraced them and helped them financially and was supportive emotionally. Being married to him brought her into a wealthier social set. She became friendly with the women of this milieu. Several of them were divorced—successfully divorced (they got a good settlement). You could see her change as time went on. The way she spoke of men in general hardened. She caught her husband in an indiscretion, or suspected it— I'm not sure which. The women were clear that he didn't deserve her, and she should get out. She did. But first, she changed who she was in that she behaved differently. She was no longer loving and caring. I don't think he divorced because he no longer loved her. I think she stopped being happy and treating him lovingly. Divorce. It's so final. There's no going back. It's almost as if she didn't think she deserved such good luck if all these women friends of hers were without their husbands.

Please be careful of those with whom you spend your time; it can change the course of your life. For an innocent woman not used to being in with the crowd, the angry women have an air of sophistication. They hold themselves above everyone—or so it seems. They look so alluring to the newly initiated of the group. There are several successful television shows about these types of women. Really, they are just hiding their unhappiness. You won't discover your happiness with them.

Take a look at the five friends that you spend the most time with. That is an indicator of where you are in your life. If you are around negative people a lot, make some changes. We tend to mirror the people around us. That's why Shanna's marriage was doomed. It wasn't her husband's fault—at least not completely. It was her friends' fault. Well, really it was her own fault. With the influence of these women, she didn't see a way for her marriage to work out.

You can get stuck feeling the very same way. Whether it's your marriage, your business, your job, your kids, it won't work out. You need to see at least a slight possibility of things working out and then visualize what it could be like as a success. What would it feel like if things worked out well? Then work the steps backwards till you get to the present. You are so powerful. What you believe is possible you can bring into being. This takes a lot of focus and concentration, and all this is about you. You don't have to say one word to him—at least not yet. Try it, you have nothing to lose.

I don't remember where I heard it. It's about planting seeds. If you plant magnolia seeds, you'll get magnolias. You won't get tulips, no matter how hard you wish for them. It you plant seeds of anger, you will get plants of anger, no matter how hard you wish for plants of love and harmony.

Now that you are willing to try a few experiments before you break up, here's the plan.

Before you get divorced, remember it only takes one to change a relationship. He doesn't even have to know that's what you're doing. Don't tell him.

Try the turnaround theory before leaving home. Meaning, if you are stuck (with anything) and the more you focus the more stuck you are, turn around so what you see is different. Stand on your head; that'll change your perspective. In fact, it will change what you are thinking. You'll be concentrating on not falling over. You might take a recess, take a vacation. But with marriage, you can stay in the marriage and move your attention inward—definitely not outward. Have sex. Have it with your partner. If sex is your form of escapism, close your eyes and ears, and have sex with your partner. Don't go outside the marriage. Not yet. Having sex with another because you are angry at your partner is the same as taking drugs. It feels good at the moment, but it ultimately adds another problem to your life.

So what do I mean by turnaround theory? Spending all this time concentrating on the marriage certainly isn't working. So *stop* concentrating on the marriage. Chill. Do something else. Here's a chance to focus on yourself, not you and the kids, not you and him, just *you*. Remember, you can't get water from an empty well. We've talked about that. You have to fill yourself up before you can be thinking of anyone else that isn't an emergency.

Make a list of things you never did, but wanted to do, and start doing them—in any order. I started with cheap and easy. I guess that tells you something about me. I'm cheap and easy. Well, I'm laughing even if you're not. I put skydiving first, but I still haven't gotten to it. But I did get to the part where I got happy without my even realizing it. That was nice. That's when I started being nice to my husband again. And I hadn't even realized that I wasn't being nice to him. He noticed the difference. It was touching—I guess I found my compassion. Notice that your list is very personal. It's just for you, to make *you* happy. Maybe you'll go to every football game, or volunteer at Ronald McDonald House. Your choice.

Now that you're feeling a bit happier, notice that happiness didn't just come to you. You worked for it by looking inside and then taking action. Feel proud. Now, frankly, it doesn't matter if you stay together or get divorced, because you are already happy, and everyone around you, including the kids, can feel it and see it.

Just remember that what you see depends on what you think is possible. What you think is possible is influenced by what you think you deserve. What you think you deserve it effected by the time and energy you put into yourself and honoring yourself with the effort to make yourself happy. And that's where your perspectives influences whether or not you stay married or get divorced. A good perspective; a good decision. That's a great place to be in your life.

Now before you take another look at your marriage, I'd like to add a few lessons to your syllabus.

No Name Calling.

Simply a cessation of name calling could significantly increase social and personal respect in the world. Tune into the news. It could be politicians, broadcasters, foreign leaders, US leaders. Keep a tally of how many times you hear them calling someone else a name. It's not the word; it's how it's used. Republican, Democrat: each is a descriptive noun, or a dirty word, depending on how it is used.

It calls into being the behavior that you DON'T want.

Once you note how common it is, start to tune it out, because, now that you are aware, we don't want that negativity polluting your everyday thoughts.

Next project for you is to track the amount of times that you (yes, little old you) are name calling, i.e., "You're an idiot," "You fat slob," "You eat like a pig," etc.

You get the idea. Write down the expressions you use, then put a check mark next to the expression every time you use it. Chances are great that you will be surprised by how much you are using that expression.

When Nathan and I first married, Nathan was pretty easy going. He was so grateful that I agreed to have his kids in our house. I didn't even realize how grateful until years later. As phlegmatic as he was, he would bristle with anger when I said, "You're an idiot to think that." I have never seen such a hard look on his face before or since (and it's been fifty years of marriage by now). His rule: NO NAME CALLING—NOT EVER. It's the only time nothing was negotiable. NO NAME CALLING, PERIOD.

As it turns out looking back, it was a good rule. I think a place that it is incredibly important is with our children. I am astounded by what I hear parents calling their children. Children are not mini-adults with thought processes like ours. They have a less developed mental and emotional system. The means that the things you—the parent, or important adult—say hit the child in the bullseye and then sink in. Children haven't learned yet how to deflect your angry name calling.

WHAT TO DO

Become aware of how much our society participates and endorses name calling. Listen to the newscast, or better yet, don't So if you have fallen into the trap, don't be hard on yourself. Never be hard on yourself; self-blame is for victims. Because we use it as an excuse to do nothing. After all, you can't help it; you can't do any better. Instead take action to change yourself. It may take time, But when you take action you are a hero, a victor. Remember the words you call yourself are as important as the words you call others.

This important technique will go a long way in improving your communication with the important people in your world. When angry, in doubt, without all the information, insecure, etc., etc., etc., BE SILENT. Silence, when coupled with listening, is a brilliant communication tool. Try it out and let me know your results. I'd love to hear your success stories at info@relationshipmiracleworker.com.

You know how when you get your appendix out, you hear about bunches of people who have gotten their appendix out? Stories you have never heard before. Maybe a more pleasant example is when you get a new car. That's what's happening to me now, as I'm writing this book. Practically every conversation somehow links to something in this book. I already mentioned that I joined Toastmasters (a communications and leadership organization). One of my colleagues gave a speech about name-calling. It was from such a different point of reference that I thought you might relate to it, and Lisa gave me permission to use her speech. Here it is.

OF COURSE YOU'RE RIGHT
by Lisa Lockhart

Have you unfriended anyone during this election cycle?

I haven't *unfriended* anyone yet, but I have unfollowed a few—not because their political views differ from my own, but because of the nastiness, name-calling, and condemnation they've heaped on anyone who disagrees with them. I'm talking about social media here, but we've all seen the same kind of angry, sometimes violent, disagreements on television and maybe even in person.

Madame Toastmaster, fellow Toastmasters, and guests, many of us in this room have opposing views, and I'm sure you're as passionate about your beliefs as I am about mine. Of course, you're right—and so am I. We can accept our differences and still get along. We know we don't need to be threatened or personally offended by each other's beliefs. What the people I've unfollowed don't seem to recognize is that they're not arguing about *facts* but about their interpretation of facts.

Each of us forms individual beliefs based on our own life experiences, usually based on preference, perception, and mindset.

For example, which way do you hang the toilet paper roll? With the paper coming over or going under? And does it matter? You hang the paper to come over the roll because your parents did it that way; or you *used* to hang it over, until a toddler or a pet—*spin-spin-spin-spin-spin*—left the paper in a heap on the floor, so now you hang it under. It seems right to you. Regardless of whether it comes over or under, though, the paper will roll *down. Gravity* is a *fact. Over or under* is a *preference.* Nevertheless, as families gather for the upcoming holidays, I guarantee you there will be intense arguments about *preferences*—the "right" way to hang the toilet paper, the "right" temperature for the room, the "right" way to mash the potatoes . . .

Here's another example you'll be familiar with. Suppose I write the number "6"on a piece of paper and set it down between two people. The person at the bottom of the page would obviously see it as a six while the person looking from the top would swear it's a nine. Yes, it is both. What you see is a matter of perspective—where you're seeing it *from.* Seeing something from another person's perspective isn't usually as simple as turning a piece of paper around. Like our preferences, our perspective is developed along the road we walk through life, including the people around us, our education, our activities, even our gender or ethnicity.

To fully understand another person's perspective, you'd have to have walked that *exact same path,* which isn't even possible for identical twins.

In general, people do what they believe is right, whether or not their belief matches our own. That's why it's so important to be kind and avoid passing judgment on people whose opinions or fashion choices or lifestyles are different from ours—because we *literally* "don't know where they're coming from."

Finally, let's talk about mindset. Most people have seen "the glass of water" demonstration: an optimist would see the bottle as half-full; the pessimist would see it as half-empty; the engineer would say the bottle is twice as large as it needs to be to hold that volume of liquid. The *fact* is that half the volume of the glass is occupied by water. The interpretation of what that means is subject to your mindset, or way of thinking. Similarly your mindset will affect the way you interpret what someone says or does.

Do you want to avoid the frustration of getting angry or offended? I'll share with you a tip that was passed along to me years ago: Before getting upset at what someone said or did, ask yourself, *What else could this mean?* Look at the facts, consider where the other person is coming from, and evaluate whether your interpretation is being colored by your own mindset. This technique can actually help you control how you feel and decide to respond.

There's a saying that you can be right, or you can be happy. I don't think you have to choose—just let the rest of us be right, too, okay? *****

Do you see how anger and name-calling affect everyone around us? And it comes from being so tuned in to what offends us that we pay no attention to what other people are feeling and thinking. Let's not take ourselves too seriously. It's one thing to be kind to ourselves; it is another thing to be self-righteous and thoughtless and/or disrespectful of other people.

Change Anger to Humor.

I think I've mentioned before that anger is a choice. Any feeling you feel is a choice. We're not used to thinking of our feelings that way, but it's a very freeing piece of information. There are a lot of ways to move from anger. Some just picture a picnic by a calm, cool rippling brook. Just saying "rippling brook" seems calming to me. The easiest way for me to handle anger, is to acknowledge to myself that I don't want to be angry. I don't need to punish him for whatever it was that bothered me. That's the biggest hurdle to overcome.

I do often think of Victor Frankl being stripped naked and then having to take off his thin, hardly noticeable wedding band and give that over too. And he, like Gandhi, refused to be defined by the enemy's savagery. They could take everything from him, but they couldn't make him think their angry, savage thoughts. He refused to match their evil. How strong and powerful as a prisoner. Once I realize that I don't choose to be angry, it's just a matter of figuring out how to change my thinking. For me, it's humor. Somehow converting anger to humor is really easy. I think it's because we all get angry at the most ridiculous things when we think about it. I will catch myself getting angry and change it to a joke. It works. (Listen, people, it'll be fifty years. I must know something.) And if we want to choose one thing, anger to humor would be a good thing to remember. Or "it only takes one"—that's a really good one too.

Another lesson I'd like to bring forward is sex. Many women complain that all he thinks about is sex, unless they complain about his never thinking about sex. But mostly, it's about too much sex. I'm not a sex therapist, so if it's a real issue with you, please do find a good sex therapist. I will share a few ideas I have that may give you a different perspective. That's my job—to give you a different perspective. Men and sex: Men are not so comfortable verbalizing their feelings. It's a big deal for them to say, "I love you," with feeling. They are more comfortable touching you, hugging you. And then they get hot. Loving you makes them want to have sex with you. I think it's biological to ensure continuance to the species. So rather than be annoyed, be flattered. Now mind you, I'm not talking about a one-night stand; I'm talking about a man in a relationship. It's really pretty cool.

Men and women are different. I know you are impressed with my genius. But once upon a time, I thought it was only physical. But it's more than that. It's the way we look at life. Actually, I think men are like dogs and women are like cats. It always makes me laugh when I say it, but as women, we tend to be coy, cool, and detached. Fortunately for us, our men are more like puppy dogs, following us around, panting. We felines take a while to warm up socially, and it takes some purposeful focus on how our bodies feel, before the feelings flow. That's just the time that it takes. Let him know he's fabulous, you're just slow, and take the time you need. Sex is meditation. Sex is a mini-vacation. Sex helps keep you healthy.

However, if a man isn't healthy, he may not be able to perform. One woman told me how angry her sick, young husband made her and how she yelled at him for not performing. I was appalled. How self-centered. How mean. Wow, could she use a lesson in compassion. There are things you can do together that can give some satisfaction and create intimacy. Check out "Becoming Cliterate" by www.drlauriemintz.com/.

If you want to know what a successful marriage grows like, I asked MaryAnn about hers. Mary Ann didn't talk about lowering her expectations; that wasn't in her head. She talked about bursting the expectation bubble. Expectations disappear. What you see before you is not your "knight in shining armor" fantasy. That Halloween costume is gone and he stands before you in stark, naked reality. What does that mean? It means he isn't driven to make a career success the way you know he should, or you expected. He isn't driven to make a million; some Uber money and a few gigs are enough for him. He has more talent than the world will ever know, and you will never be able to push him where you know he should go.

But he loves you. He adores you. He will do anything for you. He enjoys doing things that make you happy in a way no other living human being has ever loved you—well, maybe except your mother. Mary Ann's girlfriend needed to point that out to her, before she noticed how lucky she was.

Her relationship happiness comes from her appreciating the gifts he has and letting go of her expectations.

"He makes me laugh," she says, smiling to herself. Mary Ann has Cracked the Relationship Code.

PS: When I asked Mary Ann if she approved of what I wrote, she emailed: "That is so lovely! Thank you for reminding me how lucky I am. It brought tears to my eyes. Definitely use! Thanks for writing it. Xoxo."

So now that you've learned about different approaches and read about how someone created a happy relationship and life, are you ready to go back to your life, your relationship, and take another look at it? Yep, you're right he hasn't changed. But have you?

Do you see him differently? Do you interact with him differently? Do you sense a growing feeling of patience and compassion within you?

If you don't have an answer to that question yet, give it more time. And spend that time exploring what makes you happy. After all, if you quit the relationship, it will be important to know what makes you happy, so you know where to move, what job to keep, or what change or pursue. There is so much in your life that you have control of. Keep working on that and review in another month or so. If you have a clear answer, act on it. If you feel guilty about staying or leaving, that doesn't mean it's the wrong decision. It means that it's at the edge of your familiarity. What I'm saying is that guilt indicates that we are not used to this territory, this action. It's new; it's not bad. If you decide to leave, you can be more sure that it's the right decision, because you won't be subject to that overriding, blinding anger. You'll be happy about your life, compassionate with your spouse, and gracious about your exit. If you have kids, it will be easier to make decisions about them/for them/with them. You won't be poisoning their minds against him. Taking that extra time to fill your spiritual well has turned out to benefit everyone. You weren't being selfish after all; you are now giving your best to everyone—starting with you. And frankly, when you decide you're ready to explore another relationship, you will be much better equipped than you were this time.

Now you're ready to check on your job. Maybe there are some tricks you can learn that will make your job palatable, if not downright enjoyable.

Section 3

Before You
Quit Your Job

Now you're ready to focus on work. Or maybe your personal life is awesome; it's your job that's driving you crazy. Well, I actually have some hints, and I'll save the best for last, and no fair peeking.

The first thing I'd like to talk about is Edward de Bono's six thinking hats. I never heard of that till I went to Clinton Swaine's Frontier Trainings in San Diego. Clinton takes every aspect of business and makes a game of it. As you play, you gain insights and skills.

What I learned from Six Thinking Hats[2] is that there are (okay, this is going sound too obvious) different ways of looking at life, at a project, and each is bona fide. Instead of looking at the guy or gal next to you at the table as annoying and slowing down the project, I finally realized that each perspective has a value to

---

[2] http://www.debonogroup.com/six_thinking_hats.php

decision making. Edward de Bono breaks it down into different color hats as follows:

1. Blue hat (Managing): Consider the subject? What are we thinking about? What is the goal? Can we look at the big picture?
2. White hat (Information): Consider purely what information is available. What are the facts?
3. Red hat (Emotions): Consider the intuitive or instinctive gut reactions or statements of emotional feeling (but not any justification).
4. Black hat (Discernment): Logic is applied to identifying reasons to be cautious and conservative, practical, realistic.
5. Yellow hat (Optimistic): Logic is applied to identifying benefits, seeking harmony. This perspective sees the brighter, sunnier side of situations.
6. Green hat (Creativity): This perspective uses statements of provocation and investigation, seeing where a thought goes. Thinks creatively, outside the box.

Of course, if you got yourself a bunch of appropriately colored hats and acted out doing a project at work, you'd truly internalize what each style of thinking brought to the work. But just knowing about the differences and that they provided a valid input to decision making was very helpful to me—mostly with my husband.

When we've made decisions about what house to buy and such, I found Nathan to be a wet blanket on everything, and I would get angry. Then I realized that he was simply a black hat, and his job in our partnership was to be the black hat and logically identify reasons to be cautious and conservative. Clearly, I was a cross between a red and a yellow hat, so it was natural that I'd feel his pull on the reins. Just knowing he was playing a part in the decision making, and not just poo pooing every idea I had, made me respect his input and consider it.

So de Bono's six thinking hats worked for me at home; it will surely make an impact on the way you consider the people at your work. Why not list everyone and identify which hat they would wear? Next time they say something that annoys you, picture them in their appropriate hat. Just doing that reminds you that they are not disrupting the process; they are participating in the process. Notice how that changes the way you treat them and their ideas. By the way, what hat do *you* wear?

Now you know that how you perceive someone can change your feelings about them and about their competency. It may sound obvious, but it's not necessarily easy. And besides, we often think our life situation is always different from others, we think ours is worse. That's not the case.

So play this tune on YouTube to put you in the right mood to make some changes in the way you are app http://bit.ly/AccentThePostive, approaching things or people at work. This is a very old song by Bing Crosby, it gives you the entire lesson in the title: "Accent the positive; eliminate the negative."

Let's start with Eliminate the Negative. Here's what *not* to do. Now I'm not asking you to not do these things to be nice. You couldn't care less about being nice right now. Not doing these things will have a magical effect. Really. Try it.

Don't gossip.
Don't complain.
Don't participate in group griping.
Don't get stuck on who's right and what's fair. It's about what you want to create.

But wait, they always say to avoid negatives. Your brain will only remember the verb and forget the 'not.' Hmmm. So let's see if we can rework this list.

1. DO say only nice things about everyone, or say nothing.
2. DO focus on what is going well and mention those things.
3. DO avoid the group griping sessions.
4. DO put your attention on what's right and fair, rather than who's right and fair.

Remember, silence is golden. If you don't have anything to say that is constructive, then don't say anything. If you persist in thinking those complaints, change the subject in your head every time you think about "what a boob Billy Bob is." And by the way, what did we say about name-calling? Remember name-calling says everything about the person who calls the name and nothing about the target. If you get called a name, let it bounce off. It's not about you. But if you call the name, it's all about you. Best not to do it.

Well, we've now eliminated the negative. It's time to accentuate the positive. And I have a great game for you to play that will definitely change the atmosphere at work. In fact, you could do it at home as well. But right now, we're interested in your keeping your job as long as you want or need to. So this is what you do.

Make a list of everyone at work that you see on a regular basis. Maybe it's three, maybe it's ten. Okay, make the list. I'll wait. Ready? Now, number your list in a particular way. Number one is the person you like the most at work. Number two you like almost as well, and so on until you get to the end. The end is the person you like the least, or downright despise.

So here's what you do with the list. Start with number one. Give that person a compliment a day for one week (after that, once a week). Now don't give me a hard time already. It's the person you like the most. If you can't find anything nice to say about him/her, what does that say about you? Now let me explain about these compliments. They don't have to be about work. They don't have to be important. They simply have to be true—and with no strings. You can say, "I like your shirt." You can't add "for a change." Just one compliment a day to the person you like the best of everyone at your work. Okay, you've gotten through the first week without collapsing. On week two you only have to give one compliment to your bestie. But now you get to give a compliment a day to the second person on the list. And so it goes down to the last person on the list. That may be the person whom you truly despise. But look, you've had some good practice by then. You can do it. The one person I had to do that with wore expensive shoes (the ones with the red soles). I could compliment her with sincere honesty. This person may be your boss, and there are five things that you need to push yourself to observe and compliment her/him on. Remember, this is not about the other person. It's about you. By giving compliments to the people at work, you are focusing on the positive, the part that they do well. It's forcing you to acknowledge that they do something (no matter how inconsequential) right. It's the glass half full. Half full is pretty impressive to you when you thought the glass was bone dry.

Change your perception; change your life. It is astounding.

Let me tell you about my friend Patsy Bellah of Bellah Business Services. She used to work at a real estate firm in a large suite of offices. The job was fine. She was happy, except one small detail. She had to walk through another section to get to the kitchen. Everyone in that section was dour. Never a smile, never a hello. Just a cold wind. My friend Patsy was undaunted. She took this on as a challenge. Now every day, when she walked through the section, she was sure to give a big, friendly hi. Hello to the lead desk. At first, there was no response. But eventually, the woman smiled and was friendly back, and after some time the entire section was transformed. The only difference was Patsy's persistent, friendly hello. One person can change the mood of an entire section. What can you do at work?

Now you are armed with some truly great tactics to *Crack the Relationship Code* before you get married, before you get divorced, and before you quit your job. I picked those situations because that's when we tend to simply react with high emotion and low thought processes. It's when we're sure we see things clearly, but we don't even realize that we are wearing dark, dark glasses. If you know that you have some effective techniques that will help you accomplish what you want and be happy, you can relax a bit and not just react, not lash out. Chill. Take a moment. Laugh at the ridiculousness and take another look from another angle.

Epilogue

I finished the draft of this book on July 1 at 8 am. At 11 am, three hours later, I was seated with my friends at the wedding of Carla and Howard. It was a white wedding gown ceremony and the couple was beatific. It was close to an hour into the ceremony when someone read from 1 Corinthians 12:31-13:8, New International Version (NIV):

1 If I speak in the tongues[a] of men or of angels, but do not have love, I am only a resounding gong or a clanging cymbal. 2 If I have the gift of prophecy and can fathom all mysteries and all knowledge, and if I have a faith that can move mountains, but do not have love, I am nothing. 3 If I give all I possess to the poor and give over my body to hardship that I may boast,[b] but do not have love, I gain nothing.

4 Love is patient, love is kind. It does not envy, it does not boast, it is not proud. 5 It does not dishonor others, it is not self-seeking, it is not easily angered, it keeps no record of wrongs. 6 Love does not delight in evil but rejoices with the truth. 7 It always protects, always trusts, always hopes, always perseveres.

8 Love never fails. But where there are prophecies, they will cease; where there are tongues, they will be stilled; where there is knowledge, it will pass away.

I listened intently and realized that I had just written an entire book about relationship and did not once mention the word "love." Love is the last passenger on the train of relationship. First you have to release the anger and the fear, then you have to allow time in your life for another person. I think to do a book on relationship is to give you all the ingredients and then assume that you will realize that what you just cooked up is a big pot of delicious love.

About The Author

Merle M Singer is *The Relationship Miracle Worker.* When it comes to Personal Relationships, Merle works primarily with women who have relationship problems and are unhappy, or angry, or both, Merle helps them move beyond the blame to transform their relationship to a more healthy relationship– and bring more happiness into their lives! Most importantly Merle's techniques and marriage advice have been proven to work, even without your partner's participation or awareness!

Free Gift

I hope you enjoyed my book.

I believe in the Power of the Turtle --- the slow, STEADY approach to learning. It's not the "grand" move or event that turns your relationship. It's your steady, continuous focus on improvements. You can print it out or just keep it open on your mini-pad or cell phone. This focus is a recipe for a happy marriage.

I'd like to give you a gift. A copy of a book I did with my friend and partner Jay Aaron which is titled:

52 Simple Tips, Tools and Techniques You Can Do Right Now to Improve Your Relationship

The book is designed for you to read one technique a week and ease your way to a healthy or healthier relationship That gives you just enough time to read and practice one tip. Read one tip every Monday, or Every Tuesday. It doesn't matter when. I matters that you make it a habit. Giving this focus to your relationship will help restore your trust in the relationship.

You can get your copy at the website below.
www.RelationshipMiracleWorker.com/FreeGift

Bonus Chapter

So far, Cracking the Relationship Code has given you a few quick tips you ought to consider before you get married, before you get divorced, and before you quit your job.

I've spent a bit more time on the "before you get divorced" because divorce can effect more people (kids, grandparents, siblings) than quitting your job unnecessarily or hanging back from marrying.

In fact, I've created a course called, "3 steps to Transform your Relationship Experience". This course is geared to examining your current angst and relationship perspective without prejudice (meaning pre judgement). It's time to take a look at this relationship with objective eyes, as if you were a reporter.

I created a meditation audio based on the premise of a reporter interviewing a women whose husband might be similar to yours and yet doesn't seem to get annoyed at all his annoying ways—a different perspective.

Visit my website and you can down load the audio.

www.RelationshipMiracleWorker.com/guided-imagery.

Of course, I can't print the entire course here, but I have included the *10 Tools to Achieve Greater Joy and Experience More Inner Peace in Your Marriage or Relationship.*

These tools are very effective, and I've included exercises to get command of the techniques. I suggest that you read through them quickly and then, go back and practice on one Tool for a week, then go on to the next one. Mark it on your calendar for every Monday – or any day you prefer.

You can take them in any order. Start with the one that appeals to you the most.

1: Get a Perspective

Who's fault is it really that you are not happy?

Check out to see if your emotional reactions are based on an irrational belief, that your partner "should" do or not do something, say or not say something, be or not be a certain way.

List any of these expectations. Some easy examples to point to are things like how your partner squeezes the toothpaste, what he does with the toilet seat, and where he puts his dirty clothes. Other examples include what specific words that you expect him to say and what you expect him to do in any given circumstance. Does he notice when you get a haircut?

* Ask yourself: Is there anyone who, if they did this, wouldn't trigger me in the same way? If you walked into your best girlfriend's bathroom and noticed that she squeezed her toothpaste the same way your partner does, or leaves the cap off like your partner does, would you become upset with her in the same way and to the same degree?

* Actively seek examples of other women who are not triggered when THEIR partner does the same thing that upsets you. Do I know someone, or can I simply imagine the possibility that someone else doesn't become upset when their partner acts in the same way as mine?

* Ask yourself if it were you that left clothes on the floor, how would you/do you feel?

You will come to recognize that what is negative to you is not negative by the world's unconditional definition. Anybody you admire or anybody you can imagine as not being negatively affected by what triggers YOU can provide a "positive" role model for what's possible (not being triggered).

Two important outcomes of this exercise are that you...

A. Come to an awareness that you don't have to be negatively triggered by what your partner does or doesn't do. Your "upset" is triggered by YOUR unrealistic expectations based on YOUR irrational beliefs that he "should" act a certain way.

B. Accept more fully that the "solution" is to stop expecting your partner to change and instead, focus on what you CAN control: Your own beliefs, expectations, and emotional reactions/responses.

It's all about perspective and expectation. I know there is a theory that "you get what you expect," and I think there is some truth to the statement. But let's face it, I can expect to be 6"2" till the cows come home and it still ain't gonna happen, unless I learn to walk on stilts.

If you want to get what you expect, expect your partner to be different from you and that's part of his charm and part of your challenge.

2: Give Yourself to Love

When I say "Give yourself to Love", I mean relax, stop trying to control everything, and let things play out. Sometimes we women have so much invested in our marriage/relationship that we want everything and him to be perfect. Our marriage becomes our front armour plate, protecting us from the world. Sorry, Ladies, it doesn't work like that. You need to face the world head on. Your partner isn't there to make sure that you look good. No matter how close and wonderful your relationship is, we all are separate beings with separate lives. You are each there for each other to support, not judge.

The audience for RelationshipMiracleWorker.com has identified a majority of its clients and followers that are in relationship as

"25-60 year old women who blame your partner as the cause of your unhappiness **but would prefer to find a way to turn your relationship around rather than end it.**"

This presumes that somewhere inside y'all is enough love of your partner that you feel that the love that once existed is worthy of acknowledging and rescuing.

So, focus on the full part of the glass

If his wearing that frayed T shirt means to you that he doesn't care about you; the ½ empty part of the glass. Another time you notice that he does go out of his way to show you the moon when you are out and about in the evening. He does that because he knows it means something to you. It pleases you. He wants to please you.

EXERCISE

This exercise is designed to remind you of the love that you have (or had) and can aspire to once again.

Answer these questions on a clean sheet of paper:

A. What attracted you to your partner initially?

Focus on the QUALITIES that you recognized in him. Was he, for example, kind, attentive, etc.?

If your thoughts also go to "things," such as the fact that he was a good dresser, or that he had a nice car, or a good job, then dig deeper. Ask yourself: "What kind of person has those things, or does those things?" What QUALITIES did his "things" reveal or demonstrate to you about him that you found attractive? (For instance, dressing well may have represented his willingness to do what it takes to be socially acceptable.

Or not dressing well may represent that he is very focused on learning, or art or social conscious. It's not how he dresses; it's what it represents.)
B. What did you love about your partner when you first married?

Again, focus on the QUALITIES that you loved.

C. Do those qualities still exist ---- right alongside of all the stinky habits?

LOOK FOR EVIDENCE that these qualities exist, in other places than where you interpret that they aren't present.

This might be a bit difficult for some you, who are very practiced at focusing on the "negative."

Let me help You to focus on what's present now that you love, or that you would admit to loving if you gave up focusing on what you don't like about your partner.

Again, the focus of this exercise on "qualities" allows you to recognize and acknowledge those qualities more often.

Even if you like that he brings home cupcakes every now and again, this can be a reminder / trigger for your love, these events only happen sometimes, and can trigger the exact opposite emotional reaction when you AREN'T present or don't occur. If he forgets the cupcakes one week, for example.

But if bringing cupcakes is a representation of his "showing how much he cares," then the You can look for examples of how much he cares in anything and everything.

If you're having difficulty, I have a suggestion. Every time he does something that annoys you, let that be the trigger to make you focus on one thing that he is thoughtful about. Like he makes such a mess when he takes out the trash, but he does take out the trash, and that's good.

This exercise helps you by giving them your own expanded guide to the "positive" qualities that you are going to focus / re-focus on.

3: Take Dominion Over Your Anger

One of the false beliefs that many people have is: "Emotions happen TO me." In essence: "I don't control my emotions; they control me."

Letting go of this irrational but VERY powerful belief is a key to reclaiming your own happiness.

Emotions only SEEM to "happen to you" because you arise so quickly from your pre-consciousness/sub-consciousness. Your emotions are "stored" in your unconscious as habits. They're the reactions you've had to what has happened in the past, that serve as a reference point inside you for what's happening in the present and you automatically respond in a similar way. Over time, your emotions become reactions. And un-thinking reactions - whether to a charging lion or to a toothpaste tube squeezed once again in the middle - are always based in fear, and never based in love.

Anger is a special emotion, because not only is it a fear-based reaction (it's triggered by your fear that your partner doesn't love you, doesn't respect you, doesn't listen to you, doesn't care about you, etc.), but it's also a "secondary" emotion. Meaning that while anger, itself is "valid" and must be acknowledged as what arises FIRST, when you stop to examine what's UNDERLIES the anger, you discover another, primary emotion. You're angry because what happened makes you feel sad, worried, distressed, hopeless, or some other emotion that causes you pain. In some cases, it causes great pain. Anger makes you feel in control. If you really admit to the primary emotion that powers that anger, you'd likely feel weak. And nobody wants to feel weak.

There is no rule that says that you must get angry at anything.

And there IS a rule that YOU get to DECIDE whether to get angry or not. -- that you might not yet have full awareness of or even agree with,.

The path to putting this to work in your life takes two simple steps.

Do this exercise / implement this tool first as an "experiment." It's not important whether you believe the principle or believe that it will work. You only need to agree to implement it and simply observe what impact it has on them if any, and to what degree.

This exercise will be difficult for many You at first. I encourage you to keep practicing.

You must be observant, not only for measuring the effectiveness of this tool and tracking your results, but also to commit to this as a way to help them make the change you desire.

WHEN YOU GET ANGRY:

A. STOP. As in: Stop whatever you're doing. Do this by FOCUSING ON YOUR BREATHING. Take all of your attention OFF of your thoughts, feelings and judgments and transfer your attention fully to breathing in and out, deeply and consciously.

Or, equally effective, push the pause button. Visualize your pushing the pause button on your camera or computer. Keep the vision.

B. Identify what's REALLY going on inside of your emotionally. instead of staying in that anger (as appealing as that seems in the moment), identify the underlying primary emotion. "I'm upset because I'm feeling some emotion-hurt, fear, frustration.

But you must give up being right, especially, self-righteous. It's not about being right or justifying your anger. It's about observing. You're Dr Diagnosis.

When you start to "own" your TRUE emotions, you can learn to deal with those emotions (something you can control) rather than trying to change your partner's behavior, (something you can't control) or letting it trigger your anger.

This is all about observing. You can't change anything until you can see it.

4: Practice Not Being Triggered

Tool 3 helps You to "change your state" when you DO get triggered / angry.

This tool is designed to take that one step further, to the awareness that you don't have to be triggered / get angry in the first place.

Since anger arises automatically from the sub-conscious, Tool 3 helps You to "re-train" your sub-conscious habits by turning your unconscious emotional reactions into conscious emotional responses.

Once you have the experience that you ARE in charge of your emotions, you can come to recognize that you can even decide whether to have an emotional reaction to something or not.

Not being triggered is as much of a habit as being triggered is. Fortunately, even though someone has decades of practice at being unconsciously triggered, s/he can overcome that habit in far less time than it's been that s/he's had it. That's because the "negative reaction" probably only took one or two times before it became "anchored" in the sub-conscious, and after those first incidents, it's only been a repeat performance. So it may take only a few instances of stopping, breathing, and letting go of the anger that arises unconsciously before a You begins to "anchor" the NEW emotional response - which can be NO negative emotional response. No trigger. No anger.

The two options to a "negative" emotional response that gets triggered are:

1. Neutrality. (Indifference has a negative tinge.) This means that when your partner acts in a way that triggered you in the past, you simply don't get triggered. Period. Nothing happens "negatively" inside you. Nothing "positive" arises. An example would be noticing the traffic on the street, or how many people are going into the store NEXT to where you are going. It simply doesn't matter to you.

2. "Positive" emotions. This means that when your partner acts in a way that triggered you in the past, instead of getting triggered and feeling angry, you begin to feel other emotions that UPLIFT you. Or maybe you're not exactly uplifted, but you can, at least, see the humor in the situation and it just feels good but being triggered.

You can consciously create this. (Remember, YOU are in charge of your emotions.) When he does something that has triggered you in the past, simply REFOCUS your emotions on what you love about your partner. Let your love for him (even that in the past you've only felt in other circumstances) overrule and override your anger or other emotional reaction. Accentuate the positive; eliminate the negative.

Tool 5: Eliminate the Negative: Other People

You who are in this course have declared that you want to improve or save your marriage/relationship.

Making this kind of change takes more than just an intention or a thought that it's a "good idea" It takes COMMITMENT - the commitment to do what it takes to make it work.

You must evaluate what's working and what's not working in your life, and be willing to emphasize and expand what's working, and get rid of what's not working and replace it with something that works.

One of the most negative influences in a relationship and in someone's life is "negative" people. About relationships, a "negative" person is anyone who speaks negatively – especially about marriage or relationships, about your partner in particular, and/or about people of the opposite sex in general.

"Negative" talk poisons your thoughts, feelings and beliefs. It's toxic to you, and toxic to relationships.

Ask yourself: Are the negative people in my life and the negative things you're saying helping me to get more of what I truly want - more love, more happiness, more joy, more satisfaction in my relationship? This is a rhetorical question. The answer is ALWAYS "no." Negative talk by or with your friends may help you "feel better" in the moment, while you're "commiserating" with others, but it doesn't serve you by helping to improve what you're complaining about, or make your relationship better in either the short of long term.

Committing to change requires "ruthless compassion" toward others, and especially toward yourself.

One of the "ruthlessly compassionate" actions you must take is to remove negative talk - especially about relationships - from your life.

That means either:

A. *Completely eliminating one or more people who are negative—especially about marriage or relationships - yours, theirs or anyone else's*.

If someone in your life is committed to your negative beliefs and your negative talk and insist on using you as their sounding board, you may need to stop allowing them to spend time with you / stop spending time with them. However difficult this may seem, it's an essential acknowledgment of your commitment to focus on what works to get you what you want.

What you put your attention on expands. So every negative interaction expands negativity. In order to expand the positive, you've got to eliminate the negative and shift your attention to the positive.

If it's your mother or someone that close, have your interactions on the telephone and "get called away" every time the conversation turns negative. It works.

Negative people have as profound an influence on your life as friends that are drug addicts; they are very likely to pull you in.

B. Forbidding negative talk with people you keep in your life.

It's not necessary to simply get rid of everyone in your life who says anything negative.

Instead, you can declare your commitment to focusing on the positive to others, and tell them that you want your friendship to shift from negative talk to anything else. This may be difficult for them, since people like to complain so much. But if they agree to it, you'll be able to keep them as a friend (you can still complain and talk negatively to others who will allow that). And you may also notice how your commitment to eliminate the negative and accentuate the positive is affecting you and your life, and it may open them to a new possibility of how you can be, too.

People are sometimes slow to catch on and slow to change, because "habit trumps desire" every time. Even if your friends think that asking them to change your habit of negative talk when you interact with you is a good idea, you still may begin to talk negatively simply out of habit.

Your "compassionate" self may wish to allow your friends a "transition period" during which you can practice talking positively with you, and if they fall into their old pattern, you can remind them to shift their focus away from their negativity. But your "ruthless" commitment is to end negative talk as quickly as possible, so you want to give your friends - and yourself - a maximum time frame for this change to come fully into effect. If you see or talk to them often, two weeks may be an appropriate limit. If you see or talk with them less, then perhaps a month is a good time frame. Whatever limit you set, however, it's essential that you honor that for yourself. If they are unwilling to change within this time frame, you both must know that you will end your friendship with them.

There are two VERY bright spots to this commitment:

1. You'll have far less negativity and negative talk and far more positivity and positive talk in your life. With the friends you keep, this means you'll have more fun with them and enjoy them even more.
2. Everyone in your life takes up time and energy. Eliminating negative people, no matter how much you care about them, opens up that space in your life to do with as you please. You can devote the time that they took up to anything else that pleases you, including new, more positive friends. It may not feel like much of a consolation when you're in the midst of deciding to eliminate or spend less time with people who

you've had in your life for a while, but the results are well worth it.

THE EXCEPTION: YOUR PARTNER

Since you both have dedicated yourselves to improving or sharing your relationship, that commitment cannot be fulfilled by eliminating your partner from your relationship, regardless of how negative he is.

Since You also have the recognition that you can't change your partner, you must focus on your own positivity and positive talk. This will bring more joy to your own life. It may also have an effect on your relationship and/or your partner, but the direction of any effect and its intensity cannot be expected or predicted.

You get to realize that you are in charge of your own decisions. The decision to honor your relationship includes your ALLOWING your partner to be part of your relationship even though he may be negative. You are "in charge." You could leave the relationship because of his negativity or allow him to stay, out of your dedication to the relationship. This is an important, empowering perspective.

Tool 6: Eliminate the Negative: You

You may be the one bringing negativity and negative talk to your relationship.

You may talk negatively about your marriage or relationship, other people's marriages or relationships, marriages or relationships in general, or your partner. If you do, you must commit to stopping.

This is not about judgment. This is not about your being "wrong" or "bad" for any negativity you may hold or express.

It's about WHAT WORKS.

Negativity works to create dissatisfaction and divisiveness. Since You have declared that you DON'T want this, you must be willing to eliminate negativity in your own life, and replace it with positivity, which works to create the results you seek.

Like unconscious, habitual ways of reacting emotionally at the speed of thought that can be changed by bringing them to conscious awareness, negativity and negative expressions can be changed.

When you find yourself thinking negative thoughts, having negative emotions, speaking negatively, or falling into other negative patterns, simply be compassionate and patient with yourself. It's just an old pattern expressing itself out of habit that you want to get rid of.

Take a deep breath. Say to yourself, compassionately: "Oops, Change." (I did it again carried inherent judgment.) I can't wait till next time. Change is the positive trigger word that immediately switches you to positive thoughts. Let go. Replace the negative thought, feeling or words with positive ones. Move on.

Clinton Swaine of FrontierTrainings.com has a game of starting with a nursery rhyme telling the story, and every time someone says "Change" you have to change the direction of the story to practice quick changing your thoughts.

Tool 7: Eliminate the Negative: Stop Complaining About Your Partner

This tool is a sub-set of another tool, but has such importance that it's worthy of its own focus.

You care about your partner and value your relationship enough to be here.

Talking negatively about him only gives other people the impression that you don't value your partner or your relationship. Not to mention how it can "anchor" those unwanted thoughts and feelings inside of you.

It emphasizes the negative, instead of accentuating the positive.

See, the problem is, especially with friends and family who are particularly close, that you will remember everything that bothered you better and longer than you will. And when you are ready to give your love freely, you will hold you back and you will start to doubt yourself. You want you to be happy and you only know what you have said, but what you are now feeling.

So, even if there are things you don't like about your partner or your relationship right now, don't talk about them. Period. At least, give it 21 days.

Tool 8: Interact Positively With Your Partner

Relationships thrive on positive talk. Angry silence (as opposed to peaceful silence) and negativity send relationships in the opposite direction.

Everyone likes to be told how much you are loved, appreciated and respected. Your partner is no exception.

When something upsets you about your partner, hit your internal pause button. Celebrate another opportunity to practice calm. Don't say a word. Don't correct him. Simply observe and clean up. If it's the toothpaste (make a mental note to buy your own tube. If it's the trash, take it out yourself.)

Even better than speaking positively in response to something that has upset you is being proactive in expressing positive thoughts and feelings towards your partner.

One of the results of silence or saying something only when something is "wrong" is that the other person (your partner, if you do this), can create an irrational belief inside himself that you think or feel that he's "always wrong."

To counter-act this - because it's not true, of course - put significant attention on making sure that you point out to your partner every time you agree with him, and whenever you think or feel that he's "right."

By the way, communication is more than the words you say. It's how you say it, the words, you use, your gestures and facial expressions. Be genuine, congruent, generous. You don't have to give him love, but you can give him a compliment. It's what you would do for anyone you hardly know at work, or the super market.

Let him know that you don't think he's wrong all the time, and help him let go of any thoughts that he has that you might think or feel that way. By this time, the only way you can convince him that he is not always wrong is to only tell him when he's right ---- for quite a while (longer than 21 days) until your relationship is smoother and HOTTER.

Tool 9: Express Your Gratitude

Another effect of silence and negative talk alone is that your partner can get the (mis)impression that "I'm not good enough for you - no matter what I do." He can believe that he can't satisfy you. And if he feels this way in his everyday life with you, this often translates into his lack of willingness or desire to satisfy you in the bedroom or lack of confidence that he could. And also, he unwillingness to pick up his clothes or take out the trash.

Expressing your gratitude genuinely (as opposed to saying "Thank you" in a sarcastic way when that's NOT how you feel) is a powerful positive force in any relationship. More than just being positive, it can also be a healing force in a relationship.

Put your conscious attention on saying "Thank You" and "I'm so grateful for..." and "I'm so glad..." to your partner. Ease into this if you wish, or just go for the gusto.

Expand your awareness of your own gratitude and what's worth feeling grateful about. Express your gratitude for what you OR SOMEONE ELSE would find worthy of a "thank you."

Do this for yourself; not in any attempt to change your partner. Recognizing things you are grateful for and expressing your gratitude will help YOU to feel happier and more satisfied.

Even though you do this for yourself, your expressions of gratitude toward your partner may counteract any belief he might hold that he's "not good enough" for you, and that he's "unable" to satisfy you. He may become more confident and more happy. He may become more expressive of his own gratitude. He may become more open to change. Don't expect this, but certainly encourage it if you notice it.

Tool 10: BREATHE

The fastest way to "change your state" from negativity or upset is to simply bring your attention to your breathing.

If you're doing anything that requires your attention for your own safety, you must remain focused on what you're doing, of course, But to the degree that you can, you can shift your attention from your negativity or anger to your breathing as you do that thing.

If you can, it's a good idea to stop what you're doing just long enough to put your full attention on your breath, breathing in and out deeply and fully, with your eyes closed. If you're driving and can pull over for a moment, do so. If you can safely stop what you're doing for a moment, do so.

If you enjoy using "affirmations," you can combine them with focusing on your breath. But to become more calm and more powerful (meaning feeling more "In charge" and more able to consciously affect your thoughts, feelings, decisions, actions and outcomes), all that's necessary is that you become more fully "present," and all you need to do that is to simply bring your attention to breathing in and out, deeply and fully.

Conclusion

That's it. That's the 10 tools to achieve greater joy and experience more inner peace in your marriage/relationship. That's a mighty fancy sentence, but it does represent what you can accomplish if you focus. A quick word about the word, "focus". "Focus" is a double edged sword ,or word. If you focus on what a dumb jerk he is or how untrustworthy he is, everything you do and see will prove you are right.

If you focus on the things he does that are sweet, that are genuine, that are thoughtful of you, then what you see will please you. If you are pleased, you will feel happier and be nicer to your partner and everyone. That creates a warmer, more loving environment.

Focus. And be careful to focus on the roses and not the thorns.

Don't forget to get your guided imagery that will keep you tuned in to a more objective view of your relationship at http://relationshipmiracleworker.com/guided-imagery/.

And don't forget to "like" my facebook page, visit https://www.facebook.com/merlemsinger.

Happy relationship at home and work, you deserve it.

I'm always here for your questions.